JESUS, THE SERVANT KING

Six Children's Object Lessons For Lent

BY WESLEY T. RUNK

C.S.S. Publishing Co., Inc.
Lima, Ohio

JESUS, THE SERVANT KING

Scripture quotations are from the *New Revised Standard Version of the Bible*, copyright 1989 by the Division of Christian Education of the National Council of the Churches of Christ in the USA. Used by permission.

This book is a revision of *Here Is Where It Happened,* copyright 1973 by C.S.S. Publishing Co.

9307 / ISBN 1-55673-559-6   PRINTED IN U.S.A.

Blessed is the king
	who comes in the name of the Lord!
Peace in heaven,
	and glory in the highest heaven!

— Luke 19:38

Table Of Contents

Foreword

Here are six children's object lessons for Lent. The object of each is a drawing, which shows children a scene depicting the location of the story. Each lesson brings alive for children, the places where Jesus went during the critical last week of his life.

We encourage the storyteller to show the drawing of the story to the children while telling the story.

This series is not limited to Holy Week. It may be used in a number of ways. Lessons may be used for mid-week services or Sundays during Lent. The table of contents offers specific suggestions when the lessons may be used, based on the subject of the specific lesson.

The Temple

The Passover of the Jews was near, and Jesus went up to Jerusalem. In the temple he found people selling cattle, sheep, and doves, and the money changers seated at their tables. Making a whip of cords, he drove all of them out of the temple, both the sheep and the cattle. He also poured out the coins of the money changers and overturned their tables. He told those who were selling the doves, "Take these things out of here! Stop making my Father's house a marketplace!"

— John 2:13-16

Good morning, boys and girls. How would you like to use your imaginations and visit some of the places that Jesus visited during the last week of his life? If you look closely, you will see, with my help, the streets, the palaces, the gardens, the dining room, the church and even the p'ace where Jesus died and was buried.

This Lent we are going to visit six of the same places that Jesus went to, or was taken to, during the last week of his life. There is a story for each place that I think you will remember for a long time to come.

Our first picture is about the church. What do you think about when you think about coming to church? Do you think about the altar and organ? Could it be the pastor or friends in Sunday school? Some people think about prayer and hymn singing. Church is different things to different people.

I always wonder what Jesus pictured when he thought of church. Was it the tiny synagogue in Capernaum where he taught the fishermen, or was it the great temple built by King Solomon in Jerusalem? The temple is where Mary and Joseph brought Jesus as a baby and as a young boy for the high holy days. You can imagine the thrill that Jesus felt when he came to the top of the hill that overlooked Jerusalem and he saw the great gold dome on the temple. The rest of the city was built with grey stone but the dome was gold and the walls were covered with tiny smooth stones that shine in the sun. It was a beautiful sight. There are lots of places to worship God, but this place was special to Jesus and all people who loved to worship God.

When you look at the temple and you remember how much Jesus loved to come there, then you will understand the story that I am going to tell you. Jesus stayed outside the city walls at night, but he came into Jerusalem during the day to worship at the temple.

These were very exciting times in Jerusalem. Many people believed that Jesus was the person whom God had promised would come and make them a mighty nation, afraid of no one. When Jesus came into the city people followed him wherever he went. The men who were the priests at the temple did not like Jesus because they were jealous of him. They did not like it that the people loved Jesus and followed him.

At this time of the year the temple was very busy. It was always a place where men came to talk and to learn, but at Passover time there were many thousands more who visited the holy place. One of the things that happened at the church with the gold dome was that priests sold animals such as sheep, goats, doves and even oxen for men to sacrifice during worship. After they bought them they would kill the animal as a sign of how sorry they were for their sins. That was only part of the business at the temple. In the temple there were offices like a bank and you had to buy a special kind of money that was only good at the temple.

Jesus knew about these things because he had seen them, but now it seemed to be getting worse. The time when Jesus came to the temple it was particularly bad and Jesus told the people how much God disliked what they were doing. They must have made fun of Jesus or told him to leave, for before they knew what happened Jesus went into action. He took off a cord that he wore around his waist when he prayed, and he swung it in the air like a whip. With a loud voice he commanded them to leave the temple and stop acting like thieves in a

The Streets

After he had said this, he went on ahead, going up to Jerusalem.

When he had come near Bethphage and Bethany, at the place called the Mount of Olives, he sent two of the disciples, saying, "Go into the village ahead of you, and as you enter it you will find tied there a colt that has never been ridden. Untie it and bring it here. If anyone asks you, 'Why are you untying it?' just say this, 'The Lord needs it.' " So those who were sent departed and found it as he had told them. As they were untying the colt, its owners asked them, "Why are you untying the colt?" They said, "The Lord needs it." Then they brought it to Jesus; and after throwing their cloaks on the colt, they set Jesus on it. As he rode along, people kept spreading their cloaks on the road. As he was now approaching the path down from the Mount of Olives, the whole multitude of the disciples began to praise God joyfully with a loud voice for all the deeds of power that they had seen, saying,

> *"Blessed is the king*
> *who comes in the name of the*
> *Lord!*
> *Peace in heaven,*
> *and glory in the highest*
> *heaven!"*

Some of the Pharisees in the crowd said to him, "Teacher, order your disciples to stop." He answered, "I tell you, if these were silent, the stones would shout out."

— Luke 19:28-40

This morning we are going to talk about streets in Jerusalem. These streets are like none that you have ever seen before. They are narrow. Some of them are not as wide as a sidewalk and very few of them would be wide enough to drive

13

a car through. The houses where the people live and the stores where people shop are like walls on each side of the street. Only when the sun is right straight above where you walk do you see any sunlight. The streets are made of stone just like the houses, and everything in the city is grey. Around the city there is a high wall that was built for the protection of the people who lived in the city.

At all times during the year the streets of Jerusalem are crowded, but at certain times when there is a holiday the streets are so crowded it seems impossible to walk in either direction.

I want to share with you such a big day in the life of Jesus. It was the Sunday before the biggest day in the Jewish year. The next Friday was the time when Passover began and so many Jews who lived out of the city were arriving for the holy days. Jesus had been staying with his friends Lazarus, Mary and Martha at their home in Bethany. The disciples enjoyed these visits most of the time, but this visit was filled with danger. Jesus had been warned not to return to Jerusalem because the leaders in charge of Jerusalem thought that he stirred the people up and caused trouble. These leaders were afraid and jealous of Jesus.

But Jesus was not easily frightened, and he was determined to visit the temple, God's house, at this time of the year. The disciples warned Jesus by telling him what they heard. Jesus reminded them how often they wished that he would take charge and act like a king. One night after discussing the danger, Jesus made up his mind and told the disciples that he was going into Jerusalem, the walled city, on Sunday. He told them to go to a certain house and ask the man to give him a donkey's colt to be used by the master.

As I told you, the disciples did not want to go, but they loved Jesus and they obeyed him. They brought the colt to him and like a prince of peace he rode the little animal through the gate and into the streets of Jerusalem. What a surprise it was. Only a few saw Jesus at first, but they were so excited that they ran ahead to tell others. By the time Jesus reached the gate there was a crowd of people shouting words like,

"Hosanna, Hosanna!" "Blessed is he who comes in the name of the Lord, even the King of Israel." Some of the people cut down palm branches and waved them as they shouted. Others took off their coats and put them in the path of the colt and made the street like a soft blanket.

Can you imagine what it was like? Jesus riding a colt down the narrow streets with thousands of people standing and waving their palms and shouting so that the words echoed off the walls. The noise and excitement must have been tremendous. The streets of Jerusalem will never forget that day. We remember it as Palm Sunday when Jesus rode through the streets of Jerusalem to the happy voices of the people.

The Upper Room

Now before the festival of the Passover, Jesus knew that his hour had come to depart from this world and go to the Father. Having loved his own who were in the world, he loved them to the end. The devil had already put it into the heart of Judas son of Simon Iscariot to betray him. And during supper Jesus, knowing that the Father had given all things into his hands, and that he had come from God and was going to God, got up from the table, took off his outer robe, and tied a towel around himself. Then he poured water into a basin and began to wash the disciples' feet and to wipe them with the towel that was tied around him. He came to Simon Peter, who said to him, "Lord, are you going to wash my feet?" Jesus answered, "You do not know now what I am doing, but later you will understand." Peter said to him, "You will never wash my feet." Jesus answered, "Unless I wash you, you have no share with me." Simon Peter said to him, "Lord, not my feet only but also my hands and my head!" Jesus said to him, "One who has bathed does not need to wash, except for the feet, but is entirely clean. And you are clean, though not all of you." For he knew who was to betray him; for this reason he said, "Not all of you are clean."

After he had washed their feet, had put on his robe, and had returned to the table, he said to them, "Do you know what I have done to you? You call me Teacher and Lord — and you are right, for that is what I am. So if I, your Lord and Teacher, have washed your feet, you also ought to wash one another's feet. For I have set you an example, that you also should do as I have done to you. Very truly, I tell you, servants are not greater than their master, nor are messengers greater than the one who sent them. If you know these things, you are blessed if you do them. I am not speaking of all of you; I know whom I have chosen. But it is to fulfill the scripture, 'The one who ate my bread has lifted his heel against me.' I tell you this now, before it occurs, so that when it does occur, you may believe that I am he. Very truly, I tell you, whoever receives one whom I send receives me; and whoever receives me receives him who sent me."

After saying this Jesus was troubled in spirit, and declared, "Very truly, I tell you, one of you will betray me." The disciples looked at one another, uncertain of whom he was speaking. One of his disciples — the one whom Jesus loved — was reclining next to him; Simon Peter therefore motioned to him to ask Jesus of whom he was speaking. So while reclining next to Jesus, he asked him, "Lord, who is it?" Jesus answered, "It is the one to whom I give this piece of bread when I have dipped it in the dish. So when he had dipped the piece of bread, he gave it to Judas son of Simon Iscariot. After he received the piece of bread, Satan entered into him. Jesus said to him, "Do quickly what you are going to do." Now no one at the table knew why he said this to him. Some thought that, because Judas had the common purse, Jesus was telling him, "Buy what we need for the festival;" or, that he should give something to the poor. So, after receiving the piece of bread, he immediately went out. And it was night.

— John 13:1-30

It was the day before the Passover began when Jesus met with his disciples and told them that he had made a reservation for them to celebrate the Passover meal at a guest house in Jerusalem. A guest house was usually an upstairs room that people kept for special friends. Many homes still have a guest room that is kept extra nice for friends who visit from out of town. We don't know who invited Jesus to use their home on this special occasion, but we do know that Jesus must have really appreciated it.

The picture that you are looking at is not the same one that Jesus visited on a particular day, but it is the place that Christians visit in Jerusalem to remind them of this one night.

18

The Passover meal was a special dinner for the Jews to remember when Moses and the Hebrew people escaped from the Egyptians and came back to the country that God promised them. Everything they ate and everything they drank reminded them of something special that had happened to their ancestors.

Jesus loved the Passover and he came to Jerusalem every year to celebrate the great victory that God had won for his special people. On this one night when Jesus came to the guest house with his disciples it was different than any other night. It started in a very strange way. Jesus took a towel and a large bowl of water and he washed all of the disciples' feet. Can you imagine what it would be like to wash feet after they had walked in dust and dirt all day long in sandals? That is what Jesus did in the upper room. The disciples did not want Jesus to do this. It embarrassed them. Jesus was the leader, but he acted like a slave. When Peter refused to let Jesus wash his feet, he was told by Jesus that this was the only way that he could be a partner of Jesus; he must let Jesus serve him.

But this was only the beginning of that strange night in the upper room. After they ate the Passover meal, Jesus asked the disciples to listen very carefully while he told them about how he was going to share his life with them. He took a large cup that he filled with wine and some very flat bread. He told them how they should eat the bread and drink the wine after he died. They didn't want to hear about Jesus dying, but he was not afraid and they knew it. Jesus told them that when they thought about their sins and prayed that God would forgive them, God would do it. He also told them how they would receive special strength from God when drinking the wine and eating the bread and remembering why Jesus died for them and for us all.

No one ever forgot the upper room. This was the night that Judas left early and later was a traitor to Jesus. But the upper room is remembered as a holy place where God shared himself in Jesus. Look very carefully at the picture of the room. Remember that this is the place where Jesus showed us how we would receive power and forgiveness with his death and our sharing of his love with each other.

The Garden Of Gethsemane

They went to a place called Gethsemane; and he said to his disciples, "Sit here while I pray." He took with him Peter and James and John, and began to be distressed and agitated. And said to them, "I am deeply grieved, even to death; remain here, and keep awake." And going a little farther, he threw himself on the ground and prayed that, if it were possible, the hour might pass from him. He said, "Abba, Father, for you all things are possible; remove this cup from me; yet, not what I want, but what you want." He came and found them sleeping; and he said to Peter, "Simon, are you asleep? Could you not keep awake one hour? Keep awake and pray that you may not come into the time of trial; the spirit indeed is willing, but the flesh is weak." And again he went away and prayed, saying the same words. And once more he came and found them sleeping, for their eyes were very heavy; and they did not know what to say to him. He came a third time and said to them, "Are you still sleeping and taking your rest? Enough! The hour has come; the Son of Man is betrayed into the hands of sinners. Get up, let us be going. See, my betrayer is at hand."

Immediately, while he was still speaking, Judas, one of the twelve, arrived; and with him there was a crowd with swords and clubs, from the chief priests, the scribes, and the elders. Now the betrayer had given them a sign, saying, "The one I will kiss is the man; arrest him and lead him away under guard." So when he came, he went up to him at once and said, "Rabbi!" and kissed him. Then they laid hands on him and arrested him. But one of those who stood near drew his sword and struck the slave of the high priest, cutting off his ear. Then Jesus said to them, "Have you come out with swords and clubs to arrest me as though I were a bandit? Day after day I was with you in the temple teaching, and you did not arrest me. But let the scriptures be fulfilled." All of them deserted him and fled.

— Mark 14:32-50

21

Have you ever visited an apple orchard or an orange grove? This is where our fruit is grown on trees and cared for by a tree farmer. He takes care of the trees, plants new ones when the old ones die and picks the fruit to send to the markets. Not all of the fruit that grows on trees is used for eating. How many of you have ever eaten an olive? Did you know that olives grow on trees like oranges or pears?

A lot of olives that are used are grown in the land where Jesus lived. People in Jerusalem ate olives once in a while but the real use for olives in the Holy Land was mainly the oil that comes from them. People would put the olives in a press and squeeze them until they could get all the oil out of them. Then they would sell the oil.

The reason that this is so important is that one of the last places Jesus visited when he was free to walk and go where he wanted to was an olive grove called Gethsemane. Here olive trees were grown for their oil. It was not too far from the city of Jerusalem, and when you were in the olive grove you could look across the valley into the city. Many times Jesus would go there and talk with his disciples and every once in a while he would use a part of the grove as a place for prayer.

The night that I want to talk about today was one of those times. Jesus had celebrated the Passover meal with his disciples in the upper room. Then he left there to walk through the city and out of the gate, across the valley and up into the olive grove. There in Gethsemane he asked his disciples to wait while he went off and prayed. He knew something that they did not know. Jesus knew that the traitor, Judas, had planned with some of the jealous officials to arrest him. Judas did not know that the officials had a plan to kill Jesus. Now Jesus went deep into the garden and, kneeling down by a huge rock, he prayed to his Father in heaven to review the plan that he had to bring help to all the people on earth. Jesus knew what a painful and awful death it would be if he had to die at the hands of these jealous men. Several times he left the rock where he was praying to see if the disciples were all right where he had left them. They were supposed to be keeping watch, but

Golgotha

So when Pilate saw that he could do nothing, but rather that a riot was beginning, he took some water and washed his hands before the crowd, saying, "I am innocent of this man's blood; see to it yourselves." Then the people as a whole answered, "His blood be on us and on our children!" So he released Barabbas for them; and after flogging Jesus, he handed him over to be crucified.

Then the soldiers of the governor took Jesus into the governor's headquarters, and they gathered the whole cohort around him. They stripped him and put a scarlet robe on him, and after twisting some thorns into a crown, they put it on his head. They put a reed in his right hand and knelt before him and mocked him, saying, "Hail, King of the Jews!" They spat on him, and took the reed and struck him on the head. After mocking him, they stripped him of the robe and put his own clothes on him. Then they led him away to crucify him.

As they went out, they came upon a man from Cyrene named Simon; they compelled this man to carry his cross. And when they came to a place called Golgotha (which means Place of a Skull), they offered him wine to drink, mixed with gall; but when he tasted it, he would not drink it. And when they had crucified him, they divided his clothes among themselves by casting lots; then they sat down there and kept watch over him. Over his head they put the charge against him, which read, "This is Jesus, the King of the Jews."

Then two bandits were crucified with him, one on his right and one on his left. Those who passed by derided him, shaking their heads and saying, "You who would destroy the temple and build it in three days, save yourself! If you are the Son of God, come down from the cross." In the same way the chief priests also, along with the scribes and elders, were mocking him, saying, "He saved others; he cannot save himself. He is the King of Israel; let him come down from the cross now, and we

*will believe in him. He trusts in God; let God deliver him
now, if he wants to; for he said, 'I am God's Son.' "
The bandits who were crucified with him also taunted him
in the same way.*

— Matthew 27:24-44

Good morning, boys and girls. Have you ever seen a picture of a skull? How does it make you feel? Not very good. A skull is just the bone of the head, but when there are no eyes, ears, lips, nose, skin or hair, a skull is pretty frightening. I have a picture of a hill that looks like a skull. If you look closely you can see the place for the eyes, nose and mouth. That skull-like hill is just outside the gate of old Jerusalem, and it is the place where many people believe Jesus was crucified. The Bible talks about the hill called Golgotha, where Jesus died, as a hill that reminded people of a skull. Another name for this place is Calvary.

After Jesus had been sentenced to die by Pilate and turned over to the soldiers to be crucified there was a loud cheer by the people. They had been led to believe by the temple officials and other rulers that Jesus meant them harm. They told lie after lie and paid other people to lie about Jesus and the things that he did. Before Pilate sentenced Jesus to die, the soldiers had beaten him with whips that had sharp, tiny stones in them. They had made fun of him by calling him king, and making a crown for him out of thorns. When Jesus stood before Pilate they put a robe around him, but under the robe was a bloody body. People like the temple rulers, King Herod, priests and others hated Jesus because his goodness was so complete that it made their lives look evil. If the people were ever going to believe again that the evil ones were good, they had to get rid of Jesus so that there would not be such a difference.

Jesus was given a cross to carry. The cross was heavy at any time, but after being beaten, kept up all night and badly treated the cross must have felt like it weighed a ton. The soldiers led Jesus through the streets of Jerusalem where the people screamed and yelled at him, and some even spit on him.

These were the people who had heard all the things said by the priests and rulers and believed what they heard. Jesus stumbled and fell carrying the cross, but they made him stand up and continue to carry the cross, causing him great pain. Up the steep streets he walked until he fell again. This time a soldier grabbed a man out of the crowd and made him carry the cross and walk beside Jesus.

Finally they reached the hill that looked like a skull — Golgotha. A hole had been dug where they planed the cross and then, because they could think of nothing worse, they hammered nails through the hands and feet of Jesus into that cross and let him hang there until he died. They did all of this and worse. Even while he was dying they shouted insults at him and laughed at him. But Jesus never said one word back in anger to those who tortured him. Instead, even while he hung in great pain on the cross, he prayed for them, telling his Father in heaven that the people should be forgiven, for they did not know what they were doing.

It was a horrible way to die, but for you and me it is something that we shall never forget. Not even two thousand years later can we forget that hill called Golgotha or who died on it. They may have killed lots of other men on that hill, but there is one who died whom we shall never forget. He died with love in his heart for every person, even those who caused him such pain and torture. That was God's special plan. Jesus died so that our sins would be forgiven. Even the sins of those who hurt Jesus were forgiven if they asked for forgiveness, and some of them did.

Golgotha is not a very pretty place, and it has some terrible memories. But it is the place where we learned that God loves us so much that he was willing to let Jesus die for our sins.

The Garden Tomb

Now there was a good and righteous man named Joseph, who, though a member of the council, had not agreed to their plan and action. He came from the Jewish town of Arimathea, and he was waiting expectantly for the kingdom of God. This man went to Pilate and asked for the body of Jesus. Then he took it down, wrapped it in a linen cloth, and laid it in a rock-hewn tomb where no one had ever been laid. It was the day of Preparation, and the sabbath was beginning. The women who had come with him from Galilee followed, and they saw the tomb and how his body was laid. Then they returned, and prepared spices and ointments.

On the sabbath they rested according to the commandment.

But on the first day of the week, at early dawn, they came to the tomb, taking the spices that they had prepared. They found the stone rolled away from the tomb, but when they went in, they did not find the body. While they were perplexed about this, suddenly two men in dazzling clothes stood beside them. The women were terrified and bowed their faces to the ground, but the men said to them, "Why do you look for the living among the dead? He is not here, but has risen. Remember how he told you, while he was still in Galilee, that the Son of Man must be handed over to sinners, and be crucified, and on the third day rise again. Then they remembered his words, and returning from the tomb, they told all this to the eleven and to all the rest. Now it was Mary Magdalene, Joanna, Mary the mother of James, and the other women with them who told this to the apostles. But these words seemed to them an idle tale, and they did not believe them. But Peter got up and ran to the tomb; stooping and looking in, he saw the linen cloths by themselves; then he went home, amazed at what had happened.

— Luke 23:50—24:12

I have a final picture to show you today, one that you would not be able to guess unless you had been there. This outdoor scene looks something like a garden, but at the far end there is a hill with a doorway cut out of the hill. If the doorway was not so square, you might think that it was a cave in the side of the hill.

There is still a garden here today just as it was a long time ago. There really was a doorway cut into the side of the hill, but it was not the place where someone lived. No one lived there and no one was ever supposed to live there, but instead it was a place for the dead. This was a tomb that had been made for a very rich man named Joseph of Arimathea. Joseph was not only rich, but he was one of the people who made the rules for Israel. There was one big difference between Joseph and the other rule-makers. Joseph had listened very carefully to Jesus during the time that he taught in Jerusalem, and he was convinced that Jesus was the Son of God. Joseph believed in Jesus.

That is why, when Jesus was crucified and dead, Joseph asked some other officials if he could have the body of Jesus to bury. The people in charge gave Joseph the body, but told him that he would have to post a guard at the tomb to make sure that the followers of Jesus did not try to take him away. Joseph agreed, and when they took Jesus down from the cross they took him to the garden where Joseph had made a tomb for himself. Inside that doorway was a small room with a long smooth stone used as the place to lay the body. After the friends of Jesus had placed him in the tomb, under the watchful eyes of the Roman guard, they left before the night darkness came. As they were leaving they saw the Roman guard roll a very large and heavy stone across the doorway.

That's the way it stayed until Easter Sunday morning. Some women who were followers of Jesus came back to the tomb to finish what they did not have time to do on Friday night. But when they arrived at the tomb they found things to be much different than when they had left. The stone was rolled away and the soldiers were gone. When they looked inside the tomb they were even more shocked, for the body of Jesus was gone. Shocked and sad, they began to cry. But they did not cry for long, for an angel came and spoke to them telling them to go and tell the disciples of Jesus that he was no longer dead, but that God had returned him to life. Jesus had risen from the dead! Now the followers were more convinced than ever that Jesus was the Son of God.

The empty tomb in the garden that belonged to Joseph of Arimathea has been the hope of all the world ever since that day. God had promised, through Jesus, that life could be forever if we would believe in the life and teachings of Jesus. This was God's Son who had made eternal life possible by his death and his victory over death. Now you can share in Jesus' victory over death, and you can live forever, too. That's what Jesus did for you, and that is why this empty tomb is so important to you and me.

Jesus, the Servant King

Good morning, boys and girls. How would you like to use your imaginations and visit some of the places that Jesus visited during the last week of his life? If you look closely, you will see, with my help, the streets, the palaces, the gardens, the dining room, the church and even the place where Jesus died and was buried.

— From the lesson "The Temple"

Jesus, The Servant King offers six object lessons for Lent. Each lesson focuses on a place where Jesus visited during the critical final week of his life. Each lesson includes a drawing, which you may use to show children while telling your story.

The lesson themes are:
• The temple
• The upper room
• The garden
• Calvary
• The streets of Jerusalem
• The empty tomb

Wesley T. Runk is a pastor in the Evangelical Lutheran Church in America. He is a graduate of Wittenberg University and Hamma School of Theology. He served congregations in Englewood and Lima, Ohio, before founding C.S.S. Publishing Company in Lima. He has written over 20 children's object lesson books and is committed to helping congregations minister effectively to their children during worship.

9307 / ISBN 1-55673-559-6   The C.S.S. Publishing Co.
Cover design by Daniel Jankowski

house that was meant for prayer. The people ran from the temple and from the angry words of Jesus. They knew that he meant what he said. The priests were angry too, because they thought that they needed that money more than they needed to have people praying.

It makes a difference what you think about church and what church should be used for. Jesus called it a house of prayer. What do you think about church and how do you use it?

when Jesus found them they were sound asleep, exhausted from the events of the day. Each time Jesus would go back to the rock and pray and wait for his Father's answer. The answer came about the same time that he heard a noise in the olive grove.

As Jesus came into the area where the disciples were sleeping he saw Judas, some officials and some soldiers with their swords drawn. When the disciples heard the voice and confusion caused by this scene, they jumped to their feet and surrounded Jesus to protect him. But Jesus would not be protected in this way. As he asked the disciples to stand aside, Judas came up from the crowd of soldiers and kissed Jesus on the cheek. Judas did this so that the soldiers would know which one of the men in the garden was Jesus. But Judas did not have to do that. Jesus told the soldiers who he was and told them that he would go with them if they would let the disciples go. Everything was finished in the olive grove as quickly as it had started, and Jesus left, under the arrest of the soldiers.

Today that olive grove is called a garden, the Garden of Gethsemane. It is the place where once olive oil was made, where the disciples slept, where Jesus prayed and where Judas kissed Jesus and betrayed him. The Garden of Gethsemane is a beautiful place to visit today, and it is a place which reminds us of the love Jesus had for us and all the people of this world.